PREFACE

What are you really saying?

It is obvious to anyone that men and women have different approaches to life and language. A guide to what one is actually saying to the other is long overdue in order to get the most out of marriage.

Women are and always have been gatherers, and finding the best berry patch has evolved into a masterful ability to browse in shops for hours, noting items to be bought in the sales. This stamina is paramount when it comes to decision-making, such as which tin of soup to buy from the vast array now available.

Men, on the other hand, were hunters. The purpose of their expeditions into the wilderness was only for one thing at a time … wolf, bison, woolly mammoth … whatever. They caught it and then they went home. Modern man only shops for one thing at a time, as many an exasperated modern woman has observed. Also, if the one shop they go to does not stock, or has run out of the item in question, their philosophical attitude is, 'Ah well, we'll try another time!'

These fundamental differences in approach lead to difficulties and this guide may well be hailed as a breakthrough in the history of communication and as a positive boon for married couples who have been speaking, but not communicating for years.

Carol Boyd

Contents

A GROOM SURVIVAL KIT
by
Billy Simpson

A quarrel between man and wife is like cutting water with a sword
– Chinese proverb

A cynic once described the groom's view of a wedding as "a funeral where you get to smell your own flowers." Not many people seem to think much about the groom when it comes to weddings. While advice to brides is a major industry, the groom is merely a footnote at the bottom of the page.

Short of being arrested in mid-ceremony and dragged screaming from the altar by the heavy mob from the Bigamy Squad, the interest he generates is minimal as a rule. It is the bride's day.

People come to see the happy bride. The groom is just that anonymous guy in the rented suit whose pallor makes the bride's dress look off-white.

For her it is "Look this way love" click-click–click. For him it is "Excuse me are you with the wedding party?"

So why should grooms be so nervous about it if their role is merely that of a supporting player? Why should a strong man who, on his good days, could face down a rugby scrum or fight twice his weight in Zulus, become, on this particular day, a jibbering wreck whose "I will" is either a weak inaudible whisper or a panic-loud "I WILL!" that startles the preacher and convinces his new mother in-law that he's drunk.

What people tend to forget is that the groom is about to do at least two things he may never have done before. Get married and make a speech.

In these permissive times the only sexual first you are likely to experience is that you don't have to get out of bed and go home afterwards.

The thought of making a speech may be more harrowing than getting married. But either one is reason enough for panic. And at a moment when he is really in no shape for further emotional problems.

For the groom the wedding day is actually just the last straw after weeks of extensive preparations, fraught with drama and alcohol. The run up to the big day is a long series of crises, some of them real, some of them figments of the bride's fertile imagination (but no less dramatic for that).

One important piece of advice. Never hold your "Stag Night" on the eve of the wedding. A week before is better. Such occasions tend to bring out the hooligan syndrome in one's so called friends. They lose all sense of proportion when it comes to playing tricks on prospective bridegrooms.

Spiking his drink is bad enough. It is what they get up to once they get the poor wretch unconscious. Like driving him 30 miles into the country and leaving him chained to railings in a state of total nakedness.

Brides are rarely amused if the groom turns up late at the Church because the police took three hours to hack-saw him loose from the railings.

But a bridegroom should not be too well prepared in advance. Leave yourself something to do at the last minute. Even if it's only packing your suitcases. If you leave yourself with absolutely nothing to do for the last 24 hours you may find yourself afflicted by a condition known as Last Minute Dementia. Or manic second thoughts.

A mind with nothing to keep itself occupied tends to get some hysterical ideas. Like "What am I doing?" and "What times does the Liverpool boat sail?"

And it won't help if your mother goes around weeping and dragging out your old school blazer that she keeps in a shrine. Or starts showing you photographs of the girl she would rather you'd married.

The Best Man can unnerve you as well if he goes around practising his wedding speech full of witticisms along the lines of "Marriage is not a word. It's a sentence." Or "The advantage of late marriage is that there is less of it."

Don't worry ... Soon it will be
all over bar the recriminations

The Best Man is supposed to comfort the groom, not subvert him.

The wedding ceremony itself is not as big an ordeal as you'd think. For all the groom has to do he could phone it in.

Do not worry about feeling like a Zombie. Allow the best man and groomsman to lead you around and point you in the right direction. You just stand there and answer a couple of questions; pray; sing a hymn and they lead you out again.

Not many married men could tell you much about their wedding ceremony. You go through it in a daze. Don't worry. Nobody but your mother will notice. Everybody else will be focused on the bride.

Then suddenly it is all over but the recriminations.

In some ways the more trouble and nervous strain you experience on your wedding day, the better prepared you will be for life as a husband.

And anyway you will not be the most pathetic being at the wedding. That will be the bride's father who has to pay for it all. There was a time when a bride's dowry went to the groom but nowadays it goes to the caterer.

The bride's mother will probably have spent the poor soul into penury, hitting him with that old chestnut, "You can't take it with you."

To which he may mutter "I know I can't take it with me. What worries me is that at the rate you're spending it I may have to leave early."

A Bride's Tale
by
Doreen McBride

Good women always think it is their fault when someone else is being offensive. Bad women never take the blame for anything.
                                        – Anita Brookner

Our wedding day really started the night before when we had an almighty row.

It began unexpectedly just as he was about to leave. He turned to me, smiled and said, 'Good-night! See you tomorrow. Don't worry about it dear. I'm sure that whatever you do it won't matter. You're among friends and everyone will expect you to mutter your marriage vows.'

I felt enraged.

'I'm just as capable of being heard as you!' I hissed between clenched teeth.

That started it! Suddenly we were in the middle of World War Three, yelling and shouting in a frenzy of fighting ferocity. Eventually I pulled my engagement ring off my finger and flung it at him. 'Take that back!' I yelled. 'I never want to see you again.'

It bounced off the wall and hit the floor. He picked it up and slammed it down on the mantelpiece.

'I don't want that thing back,' he shouted. 'Shove it where the sun don't shine, Sunshine!' He slammed his way out of the room, banging the door behind him as he disappeared into the warm night air.

My mother rushed into the hall, visibly paled and asked, 'Is everything all right?'

'Yes!' I snarled, 'I hate him. I'm tired and I'm going to bed.'

I ran up the stairs and dropped into bed unconscious. The next thing I remember is my mother shaking me awake next morning. 'Himself is on the phone,' she announced. 'He wants to speak to you.'

I was relaxed and refreshed and, as I picked up the phone, I did not remember that I had thrown my engagement ring at my beloved and called our wedding off.

'Hello!' I said.

'Hello!' he replied, 'I'm coming. Are you?'

'Coming where?' I asked.

'To the church, of course,' he snapped, 'Have you forgotten we're meant to get married today.'

'I've remembered now,' I replied, 'I'm only up.'

'Well!' he snarled, 'I'm coming. Are you?'

Suddenly the memory of whole row came back and I felt very annoyed.

'I'm only coming because I haven't the guts to back out with all those people invited,' he explained.

'That's how I feel.' I snapped, 'That's it in a nutshell. I'll be there although I don't want to go.' I slammed the phone down.

I turned to my mother. She was loitering in the background attempting to look casual. She smiled at me in a watery fashion. I looked at her. She appeared very pale.

'Are you all right Mum?' I asked.

'I'm OK dear,' she replied, 'I didn't sleep very well last night. I was worried about you and I'm just a bit tired. I take it from what I couldn't help overhearing that you pair intend to get married today'

'Yes!' I replied, 'Although I don't want to.'

'And he feels the same way?'

'Yes!'

'Well,' she said philosophically, ' I suppose that's a good start.'

'How's that a good start?' I asked.

'You are both keeping your promises to each other even though you don't want to. In essence that's what marriage is about.'

Margaret, one of my bridesmaids went to have a bath. I sat back, looking disconsolately at my reflection in the mirror. 'Brides are supposed to be beautiful,' I thought, 'and here am I, at war with himself, my hair's standing on end and I've a spot on my chin!'

There was a sudden thump against the bedroom window sill. The window cleaner's ladder! My mind instantly sped to Margaret in the bath. The bathroom of our house had a plain glass window because it overlooked a very pretty private garden. It was nice to sit there in the bath looking out of the window and enjoying the view, the only disadvantage being it was perfectly possible for the window cleaner to look in and enjoy the view in the bath! I rushed down to the bathroom door and shouted a warning, 'Margaret! The window cleaners are on their way round!'

'I'm sitting naked in the bath!' yelled Margaret in a panic.

'I thought you might be!' I yelled back, 'That's why I'm warning you.'

Margaret had a difficult decision to make. Should she stay in the bath, turn her back to the window, wrap her arms around her body to hide her boobs, or risk a full frontal exposure by leaping out of the bath, grabbing a towel and beating a hasty retreat to my room, where there was no danger of being caught in a dishevelled state because its windows had already been cleaned. She chose the latter course of action, leapt hastily out of the bath, grabbed a dressing gown and a towel and rushed out onto the landing to be greeted by a cheery leer from the window cleaner who was in the process of washing its window.

I attempted to fix my hair. Little Felicity, the flower girl, appeared, took one look at me, turned green and announced, 'Doreen, I'm going to be sick.' She rushed to the bathroom and was - violently. The window cleaner appeared very interested, or was he interested in me as I rushed around trying to help her, dressed in nothing but my slip?

Bill, my father, had hysterics. 'We can't have a child boking all over the wedding party,' he announced. 'Get her out of here.'

'Hush dear!' comforted mother, 'She's probably finished. She's just over excited.'

Mum 'phoned Aunt Emma who confessed that Felicity had a tendency to throw up before big events, but, having expressed herself, settled down and enjoyed the occasion.

'Felicity, what do you want to do?' I asked.

The response came quickly, 'Wear my pretty dress and carry my basket of flowers up the aisle with everyone looking at me.'

I thought any deflection of attention away from the bride sounded like a good idea although Mum came and managed to fix my veil over my hair so that only the bit nearest my face stuck out. The spot shone like a lamp so I scribbled over it with some concealer and thought, 'I don't know why I'm worrying. I'm doomed not to be a beautiful bride. If the weather turns cold I'll go blue and become covered in goose pimples, while if it's warm my make up will melt, stream down my face and leave my spot glowing like a beacon.' Oh! It would be lovely to be the groom and be comparatively invisible!'

I stood up, dejected, as Felicity came back into the room. She was wearing her pretty pale pink dress with its white lace edged flounces and was obviously thrilled with her appearance. She caught sight of me 'Doreen!' she gasped, 'You look beautiful! Nearly as nice as me!' I laughed and as I did so glanced out of the window. There was himself standing on the steps of the church opposite with a huge smile on his face as he posed on the steps for the photographer. 'Hypocrite!' I thought.

The bridesmaids departed leaving Bill and me standing alone in the hall. It felt like death. Shocking silence, where a moment ago there had been bustle and laughter.

The wedding car arrived. I sprockled in, veil and all. Bill passed male type judgement on my apparel. 'That bloody veil's a bloody nuisance!'

'Where are we headed?' asked the driver.

'Osborne Park Methodist Church, just across the road,' I replied.

'I thought she could walk.' Bill stated in an emphatic fashion, 'And save the price of a car. Himself agreed with me.'

'I thought if it rained I'd be soaked by the time I got down the drive and across there.' I explained.

'Quite right,' replied the driver. 'I agree. Tell you what. We'll pretend we had to come a distance. I'll drive out onto the road, turn right, go up the park and around the square. It'll feel better.'

I agreed, but some of the wedding guests looked alarmed as we drove past them and disappeared from view.

Panic set in as Bill and I stood at the church door waiting for the signal to walk up the aisle. The lights flashed to tell Leslie, the organist, we had arrived. He also appeared panicked. I could see him searching the top of the organ with one hand while continuing to play with the other. Music cascaded off the instrument and hit the floor. Bill stuck his right foot out and stood there, waiting, like a penguin.

'Get your foot up and let's see if we can get this walk in time,' he bossed. 'Remember to go slowly so it doesn't look as if you're getting married in a hurry. He looked as if he was in his element.

Men are funny creatures. Most, if pushed, admit to longing for a daughter, then they look forward to giving her away on her wedding day and they feel disappointed if they are denied this experience! Of course, male style, they are dishonest about their feelings and complain about the whole business.

I obeyed Bill's instructions, lifted my right foot and, as I felt like a fool I giggled. Friends turned round and smiled, happiness flowed through my veins. I saw himself standing with his back to the congregation and love cascaded out of my heart. The wedding march started. The wrong one, but never mind. Later Leslie confessed he momentarily lost the wedding programme on top of the organ so I proceeded up the aisle to the wrong tune. Strangely enough I did not feel it was the wrong wedding. That came later.

I reached the altar sustained by smiles from friends and family. Himself turned round. I smiled, straining my ears to hear what he would say on this momentous occasion, the day of our

I was sorry I did not have the foresight to include 'Fight The Good Fight' among the hymn tunes to be sung

wedding. Would he tell me that he loved me? Would he say that I appeared beautiful in his eyes? Alas no! Himself turned round, glowered and said, 'My feet are all covered in mud.'

'Your feet are all covered in mud?' I repeated incredulously.

'Yes!' he snarled.

'Why are your feet all covered in mud?' I asked, suspecting that few couples have ever indulged in such an unromantic conversation at the altar.

'Because Belfast Corporation decided to dig up the drains outside our house before the wedding car arrived. I had to climb over their earthen works to get into the car.'

That did it! I remembered the previous night. I remembered the row. I remembered he had the cheek to suggest I would not be heard behind a tram ticket. The sod! In retrospect I felt sorry I had not the foresight to include 'Fight The Good Fight' among the wedding hymn tunes.

I heard him make his first response in a quiet voice. My turn came. I bellowed the reply.

Himself gazed at me in amazement. 'The cow!' he thought. 'She's determined to sound louder than me. She remembers we aren't speaking. He yelled his next response in a voice that would have done credit to an army major. Later, at the reception in the then Conway Hotel, we were amused to be told that we had spoken up 'like men' and that we sounded 'very sincere' as we took our vows. We felt we had made an awful mistake. That 'mistake' has lasted over thirty years, in spite of the fact that the three piece band, hired to provide background music during the reception, played as their first piece, 'I'm Just a Fool Who Can't Say No'!

I agree with Billy. If panic sets in a few days before your wedding, ignore it – the panic, that is!

The Opposites Theory
by
Billy Simpson

*The great question which has never been answered and which I have
not yet been able to answer despite my thirty years of research into
the feminine soul is what does a woman want?*
— Sigmund Freud

One of the popular theories for the apparent incompatibility of
many married couples is that "opposites attract".

Don't believe it. Women get more opposite as they go along.

As a fiancee, a girl may giggle delightedly when her future
husband gets a little high at parties; puts a lampshade on his head
and does his Tommy Cooper impersonation. The same
performance by a married man wins him a kick on the leg and
the admonition "Sit down y'ejit. You're making a fool of
yourself".

Husbands tend to get kicked in the leg a lot at parties. Usually
at the first sign that they may be enjoying themselves.

You can tell how long a man has been married by counting
the notches on his shins.

All the wildness and frivolity that you thought attracted them
to you in the first place when you were a bachelor-about-town
seems to become a major embarrassment once the gold band is
on the lady's finger. Character defects that she devotes the rest of
her life to ironing out.

Sadly men dislike what they regard as their best qualities being
ironed out of them - but as an aid to survival invariably curb their
wilder instincts in the presence of wives. Which leads other
women to gloat admiringly "She's fairly settled him down", as if

intimidation is an acceptable substitute for willing submission.

At country funerals you can probably still hear women mourners make the traditional remark "Ach sure he was a wonderful, quiet wee man. Sure you wouldn't have known he was there half the time."

Presumably, for women, invisibility is an important character plus in a husband.

He was a wonderful, quiet wee man

A Right Fiasco
by
Doreen McBride

Macho does not prove mucho
– Zsa Zsa Gabor

It is amazing how men become invisible when they are needed. If you are out on a shopping expedition and need advice your special man will disappear into the crowd. If wee Johnny falls down and breaks his arm as you go into labour you can guarantee that he will be nowhere to be seen.

Himself and I go back a long time so this particular fiasco happened in the late 50's when we became engaged to be married and did the rounds, being introduced to each other's family. Personally I should have been warned the day himself took me to see his mother's Aunt Aggie who lived near Ahoghill.

Aunt Aggie lived in a traditional Irish cottage. She was well into her eighties and as sprightly and pleasant an old girl that I ever had the privilege of meeting. She was as bright as a button, with her own philosophy about the meaning of life. She did not believe in what she called 'new fangled contrivances' so lived without what she considered to be the dangers of electricity, running water and proper sanitation.

I was made very welcome, given a stick back chair beside the fire and a 'wee cup of tea in my hand' with a piece of fresh warm soda bread, which had been baked on the griddle over the fire that morning and was now smothered in delicious country butter and strawberry jam. Himself disappeared over the fields with his cousins leaving me beside the turf fire, with its old crook and crane, a couple of old men and Aunt Aggie. She threw some coal among the turf and the chimney began to smoke.

The old men and Aunt Aggie appeared oblivious of the smoke but I began to cough while Aunt Aggie confessed that there was one modern contrivance she was thinking of adopting, a tricycle.

'Could I get a big tricycle?'

'Why do you want one?' I spluttered.

'It's like this,' she replied, 'It's a long way to the shops and I don't know what's wrong with me. I had a wee bit of a fall in June and sometimes I'm no too steady on my feet. I tend to wobble on my bike. If I was on a tricycle and had a giddy fit I could just hang on to the handlebars and wait til I came til.'

At that a great cloud of smoke belched down the chimney enveloping everyone in the room. It was too much for me. Instead of attempting to hold a conversation and not cough I was suddenly helpless, overcome with a paroxysm of choking. Helplessly I choked, coughed and spluttered, growing red in the face and gasping for air.

'She's not used to the stir.' Aunt Aggie pronounced as she placed her arm around my shoulder and guided me through the dense smoke to the pure air outside. We stood at the door, admiring the gentle landscape with its green trees, wild flowers and scented hedgerows.

'It's quare and different in the city, isn't it?' asked Aggie.

'You're right there,' I replied. 'Have you ever been to the city.'

'Once!', came the quick response, 'And I've no notion of going back. The air there was awful. Stinkin' it was!'

I was interested in the tansy she had growing outside her door. She explained that it was an old plant which she used to keep the flies out of the house, to keep moths from destroying her clothes and to flavour white sauce for fish. Then she leant against the wall and we listened to the birds singing and I could not help hearing the old men inside discussing me in unfavourable terms.

'That poor misguided lad!' I heard one old man say, 'He's got the quare bad bargain with thon wee woman.'

'Aye!' replied the other, And it's no good telling him 'cos the young ones will nay listen.'

'You're right there! They've no sense an' ye could nae talk til them!'

'Cud ye just see yon wee woman in a field!'

I felt very indignant. There was no way I was going into a field with either of those guys. I was a 'townie' and I had my virtue to look after..

There was a hearty burst of laughter inside the house. 'Sure she'd be no good. She couldn't pull a plough, her back's not broad enough.'

I was reminded of an advert placed in an Irish Farmers' Journal. 'Bachelor farmer, with good thresher seeks strong healthy spinster with a good tractor, with a view to marriage. Send photo of tractor.'

My thoughts were interrupted by the conversation inside the house. One old boy was saying, 'Did you hear her cough? She'll be dead within a year of the consumption.'

I looked up in concern at the thought of impending doom to find Aggie smiling at me in a kindly fashion. 'Don't pay any attention til them auld fools,' she said. ' They're talkin' out of their left ears. You're like me, wiry, and wiry ones last. I've seen all my friends who were big women, under the sod. I sure felt sorry for big Bella.'

'Who was Big Bella?'

'She was my best friend.'

'What happened to her?'

'She went and married Bert. Sure he wore her til a frazzle and she wur dead within five years. Mind you, he was a dirty auld brute. "Bella!" he used to gulder every day after he'd had his breakfast in him, "Git up them thar stairs! I want til give you a poke before I go out and milk them thar cows." He refused til milk the cows unless Bella had a poke! Wore her out he did.! Him and his pokes! He gave her four children in five years, then she died. Wore out she was!'

'Oh dear!' I replied. 'What happened to him and his poor motherless children?'

'Thon man's a survivor. The more I think about it the more I realise men in general and Irish men in particular, are survivors. They find a cow more difficult to replace than a woman anyday. Well, Bert went and made sheep's eyes at Sally and the poor ejit fell for it and married him. He wore her out as well and now he's on til Lizzie. Lizzie's lasting rightly. She's older and a different kettle of fish. She probably tells him what he can do with his poke!'

I was really puzzled. I was young and innocent, lacking in worldly knowledge. To me a poke was an ice-cream cone! How could a woman be worn out because she kept being offered ice-cream? And where was himself when I was being insulted and having my innocence assaulted? Over the fields with the fellows, that is where. And where is he now when he is needed? Goodness knows! He can be under my feet one moment complaining about needing food, yapping about the pangs of hunger, complaining that his belly thinks his throat is cut, insisting he is dying of starvation. Where is he when the meal is finally served a minute later? Gone, that's where.

THE TRUTH IS OUT THERE
- SO IT CAN'T BE IN HERE
by
Billy Simpson

*Having a woman around the house is a bit like having a mystery
novel with the last page missing*
– Billy Simpson

Women often ask each other "Why do men lie to us so much?" A
man would say, "Because you ask so many bloody questions."

Of course men lie to women. Not necessarily from a desire to
deceive. More from an instinct for self-preservation.

From the newlywed's first attempts at cooking
"Don't cry. Of course it's not a disaster. If we
scrape the burnt bits off it could be quite tasty."
Which in manspeak means "If this doesn't kill me the
stomach pump might."
And "No. Of course that dress doesn't make you look fat."
Which in manspeak means "It's the extra two-stone that makes
you look fat."

A woman is a walking question mark. She will ask a man
questions Jeremy Paxman wouldn't ask. From the deeply personal
to the trivial. From "What's that you are writing in your diary?"
to "What did you have for lunch?"

A man's life is a constant cross-examination with big important
questions hidden in there amongst the gush of trivia.

Some of them he should never answer. One in particular.

At some moment in every marriage a woman who has been
quietly reading or just staring at the fireplace will suddenly ask
her husband the killer question.

"If I died," she'll sigh, "Would you marry again?"

Do NOT answer this question. It is one of those questions that there is no safe answer to.

If you say "No", she'll narrow her eyes and ask "Oh, so marriage to me was so terrible you'd never do it again?"

If you say "Yes, I would marry again," she will go quiet for a moment and then enquire icily, "WHO?!!!!" Assuming you already have a substitute warming up on the bench.

You imagine the answer "Maybe" would get you off the hook. It won't. It gives her imagination two sticks to beat you with instead of one.

They will never say so, but, ideally, a woman would like to think her husband would be so distraught at her funeral, he would throw himself on top of the coffin and sail into the flames of the crematorium with her.

When a wife asks this killer question, find some way of distracting her. Fake a heart attack if necessary. If that doesn't work, have a real one.

Believe me, it will save a lot of aggravation in the long run.

The sociologists are right about one thing. Problems of communication cause marriage breakdowns. There is far too much communication. Less would do.

The trouble is neither the marriage service nor prenuptial agreements say anything about equal air-time. In the main a wife tends to be the communicator and the husband the communicatee.

A woman can communicate in mysterious ways. One of their favourites is telepathy. She will start a conversation in the middle and get annoyed when you don't understand what she is talking about. The first part of the conversation was in her head and only the second part verbalised. It's like going into a cinema in the middle of the movie and trying to guess what has happened before from what is happening now.

When a woman is thinking over what she wants to say to you she will often rehearse the scene in her head. Inventing your end of the dialogue as well as her own. Sometimes she won't like something you say in these little playlets running in her imagination and get irritated with you over an insensitivity you have not yet had the opportunity to commit.

Many a man has glanced up from his newspaper of an evening and been startled to find his wife glaring at him with cold eyes over a wrong word in a dialogue he wasn't even in.

Suddenly she'll snap "Well!! Is it Yes or No?"

You haven't a clue what she's talking about but do the normal manly thing. Bluff. Just in case you were reading when you should have been listening.

It's a fifty-fifty chance at worst.

"Yes," you say, but from the look on her face you guess you have guessed wrong.

"I mean No."

"No What?" she'll say.

"er... No SIR?"

It can't be accidental that the boom in agony auntery in the media has coincided with the sharp increase in divorce statistics.

You will have noted that it is invariably agony aunts rather than agony uncles. If it were agony uncles giving the advice there would be a lot less of it.

And none of it would include anything about partners being totally honest with each other. A man would never advise anybody to try bringing total honesty and frankness into marriage.

The marriages that survive are not those where husbands go around pouring out their feelings. They are marriages where husbands know when to shut up and allow their wives to do the pouring.

Men have learned to nod understandingly from time to time. Often long after they've stopped listening.

Women are natural communicators and have an obsessional need to analyse everything under an emotional microscope. The average man does not have the same overpowering compulsion to verbalise his every thought.

A man learns from sharp experience that the less of his feelings he articulates around the house the better his chances of getting through the day without any dramatics.

There was a case in the United States a few years ago where a man was advised through a radio phone-in to sit down and talk frankly and honestly with his wife about each other's faults. He must have listed one fault too many because while he was still opening his heart to her, she got a knife from the kitchen and tried to open his liver as well.

For agony aunts to advise total strangers on the basis of a brief letter or phone call is really playing poker with somebody else's chips. There is a temptation to take risks you wouldn't take if it was your own money.

All this nonsense of talking through your problems with total honesty started in America. A country where one citizen shoots another every fourteen minutes.

So fourteen minutes would seem to be the extreme edge of endurance for listening to total frankness before becoming homicidal.

THROW BANANAS THROUGH THE BARS
by
Doreen McBride

A little alarm now and then keeps life from stagnation
– Fanny Burney

Daphne, not Billy's long suffering Daph, but another good friend, appeared in bad form. She looked tired and dispirited, not her usual bubbly self. 'What's wrong?' I asked.

'I must be the last virgin left in Ulster.' she moaned, 'Here I am, in my sixties overweight, with high blood pressure, bad feet and troubles. Yes! I know we all have troubles but I have no-one to share them with. Every night I go home to my lonely pit without a single soul to talk to. I used to enjoy my freedom, now I'm beginning to envy married friends. They go home to the comfort and support of a husband and it must be nice to have a pair of arms around you and a bit of chat when you are down.'

That would be nice! Why does marriage not work that way? Why is it that whenever a woman is feeling down her dearly beloved buries his head in a newspaper and sits and grunts? At best she will be told not to worry, to catch herself on, or be regaled with a list of his woes so that she not only has her own problems to contend with but also has his. It is no wonder that psychologists say that the happiest people on earth are single women.

My friend Ernie reckons that men do not mean to appear unsympathetic to women. He thinks men and women are two different species. They simply do not understand each other. 'Mixed marriages are known to suffer from difficulties,' he says, 'so human marriages are bound to cause trouble because it is conventional for a man to marry a woman. In other words, it's a mixed marriage. It's doomed from the start. It would have been much more sensible if nature had arranged things so that a man could marry a man and a woman could marry a woman. They would have had much more in common and would have understood each other better.'

On reflection I am inclined to agree. Take the way men and women respond if they are worried. A woman wants to talk. Will the average man listen? No he will not! I remember coming home after a hard day at the beginning of a new teaching year and confessing, 'I'm exhausted. I've had a rotten day. I'm worried because I think it's going to be an awful year. My best friend has found a lump and is sure she's got cancer. One of the men sexually harassed me. My teaching time-table is grossly overloaded, I'm teaching every lout in the school, my practical classes are so large they're above the legal limit, I haven't enough equipment to deal with them and I'm teaching in a hut outside. It's ghastly and the playground around it floods so I'll have to paddle out to it in bad weather. It'll be terrible in the winter. I think suicide's the only way out!'

Himself had his nose buried in a book. He grunted in a good imitation of a baboon. I repeated my troubles at the top of my voice and received another grunt in reply. It was obviously time for drastic action. I grabbed the book from out of his hands and shrieked, 'Will you LISTEN to me?'

He looked up and asked, 'Is there anything wrong dear?'

Why do men ask if there's anything wrong when it is patently obvious that your troubles are about to cause a nervous breakdown? If a comet should collide with the earth, shaking it on its axis, causing all sensible women to go into hysterics, the average man would turn to his wife and ask, 'Is there anything wrong dear?'

I explained the whole scenario once more. Himself looked annoyed. I had taken his book from him.

'I was sexually harassed!' I yelled.

'The fellow must fancy you.' came the quick response, followed by a slightly worried, 'He's not likely to get anywhere, is he?'

'Yes!' I shouted, 'Buried!'

'That's all right then!'

He attempted to retrieve his book. After all it was interesting, but I was having none of that. I insisted on expressing all my concerns. Himself listened, thought about it, then offered a solution. 'That job,' he said, 'appears to be a dead loss. Why don't you resign?'

Resign? How could I resign? We had a mortgage, an overdraft, we needed a new car, the kids enjoyed optional expensive extras such as music lessons, ballet and verse speaking. Resignation was out of the question. Why do men have to add to a woman's troubles by suggesting unrealistic solutions? Why can they not realise that all they need do is offer the kind of help that is freely available from another woman? All that is required is a listening ear. A sympathetic hearing and a bit of a cuddle work wonders.

It is an entirely different scene if a man has problems. He does not want to talk. He retreats into ancestral folk memories of living in a cave and he bears a passing resemblance to an ape as he loses the power of speech. He sits there, lost in his own misery, grunting like a baboon, annoyed by any attempt to communicate with him and liable to snarl at anyone who comes within ten yards.

Himself normally has a pleasant humorous personality and the baboon side did not appear until we had been married about six months. Suddenly he regressed. He sat and snarled and refused to discuss anything. I realised he was worried and tried to comfort him. I tried to get him to talk to me, did my best to appear sweet and understanding then having suffered for three weeks I lost the rag, turned into a raging virago, told him exactly what I thought of him and went shopping. When I came back he was smiling. I looked at him in surprise. 'What's wrong with you?' I asked.

'Nothing.' he replied.

'That's what I mean.' I said, 'What's wrong there's nothing wrong? You've been like a bear with a sore head for ages.'

'I'm sorry. I was worried. Now I've worked it out I feel better. Boys-a-dear I didn't know you knew all those bad words!'

Smile at your enemies,
it drives them mad!

'Neither did I!' I laughed, 'Tell me something, why did you appear annoyed when I realised you were worried and tried to help, yet the minute I lose the bap and swear at you, you recover? It doesn't make sense.'

'It doesn't make sense to a woman, but it makes perfect sense to a man. I was worried and thinking. When you tried to talk you disturbed my thoughts. That was irritating. Then when you were nice to me I felt annoyed. There's nothing more annoying than somebody being reasonable when you're cross! You know the old saying, "Smile at your enemies, it drives them mad!"'

'Right!' I said, 'next time you go moody on me I'll pretend you're a bear in a cage, feed bananas through the bars and go out and enjoy myself.'

He laughed, 'That sounds fine. Just keep the food coming and enjoy yourself so I don't have to worry about you.'

Himself has also learnt how to deal with my troubles. If I say, 'Look here, I've either got to talk to you or find something constructive to do,' he sits and appears to listen. That, to him, is the lesser of two evils because once, when I was feeling worried, he told me not to bother him, as he was busy. I should catch myself on, be sensible and go and find something constructive to do to divert my mind. I knew he was preparing for exams and felt he was probably right. I should go and find something useful to do so I went into the bedroom and started stripping the wallpaper off the walls. He was horrified when he found I had taken his advice and was glumly attacking wallpaper. That was a good move in more ways than one as the place was badly in need of redecoration and it taught him to listen! My friend Jan adopts a similar attitude. When she is really troubled she goes and stands in front of her husband and yells. 'I need attention. Open your ears, read my lips and LISTEN!' When Gerry shows signs of trouble she, like me, just keeps the bananas going through the bars.

"IT'S IN THE WASH," SHE LIED
by
Billy Simpson

There is a vast difference between the savage and the civilised man,
but it is never apparent to their wives until after breakfast
— Helen Rowland

In Spring it is never safe to leave a woman alone with her imagination. They do not see Spring as a time for Hey Nonny No-ing. They see it as a project. Something to be attacked, hacked, mowed, scrubbed, painted, refurbished, cleared out and - if necessary knocked down and re-built.

The season does something to their vocal cords that compels them to emit a screech of displeasure at the sight of a man in an armchair.

And more than anything it makes them deceitful, ruthless and conspiratorial. Just how deceitful, ruthless and conspiratorial I discovered by accident when Carol, a friend of mine, inadvertently supergrassed on the sisterhood.

I refer to the Sisterhood of the Black-Bag.

When a man comes home and finds several large plastic bags of stuff tied up in the hall and enquires "What's in the bags?"

"Nothing" she says furtively, "Just some rubbish for the dump."

"There is nothing of MINE in there, is there?"

"No there isn't" she insists. Sometimes accompanying her denial by widening her eyes, having read somewhere that this denotes innocence.

Before the invention of the black plastic binliner a man had an even chance of rescuing a favourite garment or some sentimental little nick-nack from the bin, before the bin lorry got to it.

But the black bag hides a multitude of sins and tearing one open to check her denials has been known to cause the occasional domestic crisis that could end in tears. Or even bruises.

Inferring that your wife is a liar can be a brave, even heroic act. Since the words bravery, heroism and husband are not an entirely compatible trio, we tend to take their word for most things.

A big mistake. Women in black-bag mode will throw anything out. They have absolutely no sentimentality about a husband's possessions.

Particularly old clothes that he has grown fond of over the years.

Women sometimes refer to such garments sneeringly as "His security blanket." As if holding on to garments that have holes in them is neurotic.

Then they disguise their vandalism by spacing out the remaining hangers in the wardrobe to make it look as if nothing is missing.

When a man goes hunting for his favourite old cardigan, or whatever, and enquires as to its whereabouts, she has a ready answer.

In fact several ready answers, which she recycles from time to time.

"It's there, you just can't see it."

"It's in the wash."

"I'm sewing a button on it later."

In truth you will never see that garment again. It is either buried in a skip~ hanging in the Oxfam shop or part of the foundations of a factory at Duncrue Industrial Estate.

Women are even more troublesome when they begin to tidy

up the home. Every home should have a shabby corner. Even shabby homes should retain one corner that is even—shabbier than the rest. This is a philosophy I have come up with after 30–odd years of marriage and home improving. Wives tend not to go along with this theory, believing any part of a home, either interior or exterior, below the mean average of the rest of the house should be brought up to scratch. Cleared out, cleaned up, decorated, replaced altogether or otherwise tarted up.

This is a mistake.

Bitter experience has taught me that the rest of the house only looks good when there is something shabby to compare it to. Once you tart up a shabby corner it invariably looks better than the rest of the house and instead of having one small area of shabby, you wind up with the major part of the house taking on a neglected look.

Anyone who has ever touched up a mark on a door frame with a dab of paint, knows what I mean. Suddenly the touch-up makes the rest of the frame look discoloured. Paint the frame and the door looks discoloured. Paint the whole room and it makes the furniture look shabby. And the hall and all the other rooms.

You are caught up in an endless spiral of Ideal Homery that keeps DIY stores in profit and families either in debt or injury time.

In fact having an area of shabby is the only thing that makes the ordinary look good. This is the ultimate proof of Einstein's theory of relativity. I suspect it may have been home decorating that gave him the idea in the first place.

Sometimes it is better to let well alone. Not to go striving for perfection all the time. Perfection is an expensive dream and impossible to achieve.

And having all the money in the world would be no help.

Entertainers like Michael Jackson and Cher are not short of a few bob but they made the mistake of being unhappy with the looks God gave them and started off by having their noses fixed. Then they discovered that the new nose looked better than the face it was on and had the face improved. The new face made the body look a bit second hand so they carried on until now they daren't sit too close to the fire in case they melt all over the fender.

And a woman with silicone breast implants risks exploding if she flies on an aeroplane above a certain altitude.

Leaving well alone is not a fashionable philosophy in these frenetic times. We are becoming a society of control freaks.

Imagining that anything that looks lived in should be sanitised to meet some fantasy idea of perfection.

Sadly, in a untidy world, perfectionists are doomed to live their lives in a constant state of agitation and cruel disappointment.

Utopia is one of those places you can't get to from here.

Instead of living in a perpetual fret about the fact that some things don't look as good as others we should be using old Albert Einstein's relativity theory to take advantage of the contrasts. Like the pretty girl who always has a homely girl as best friend. Or the politicians who always strive to stand beside David Mellor in a group photograph. The contrast can make them look better than they really are.

You can't get to Utopia from here

SOCK IT TO HIM - HIS WAY!
by
Doreen McBride

The wages of sin is alimony
Carolyn Wells

Billy believes we are becoming a society of control freaks and that we should leave well enough alone. Strangely enough, I agree with him.

As a new bride I used to be really worried about socks. I did not understand them. What do they do once they leave feet and are put into the wash? They go into the laundry basket as pairs and come out of the wash as singles. I have come to the conclusion that being cleaned must be an extremely stressful occurence for socks, leading to what must be the highest divorce rate in the world. Daph says she has the same trouble with Billy's socks and we know, from intellectual discussion with other women, that we are not alone.

I used to attempt to control socks, conscientiously counting pairs as I put them into the washing machine, then attempting to count them again as I took them out, hung them on the line in pairs and finally folded matching socks together as I put them in the hot-press. I inevitably ended up with a goodly proportion of singles, in spite of all my loving care and attention.

Himself, male fashion, contributed to the general confusion by taking his pairs of socks out of the hot-press, swearing at them because they were neatly folded together, unfolding them so, he said, they were ready to wear, then putting them in a large tin.

One day himself was in bad form. He took out his sock tin and could not find a single pair. He became enraged and blamed me for stupidity, saying that I could not even manage a simple job like washing socks without turning it into a disaster area, so that he did not have a single pair of socks.

"Right!" I replied, exasperated "As I am so useless, the next time you need clean socks, wash them yourself. That way there should be no mistake. I'll switch the machine on for you, and let's see how you do!"

Strangely enough, the divorce rate between the various pairs of socks was even higher than usual. Himself was really puzzled by this turn of events, then made a momentous decision. In future he would possess nothing apart from plain black socks, then if the rascals became promiscuous in the wash it would not matter and errant partners could eventually meet up again without anyone being the wiser. They could quietly practise serial monogamy.

As for me, I have learnt over the years not to try so hard. There is no reward for virtue. Now I just throw socks into the wash, do not bother to try and sort them and thus save a lot of time. Sock it to him his way. That has become my philosophy and I recommend it to new brides.

Dot says Roger began married life as a husband from hell and that it took a lot of time, devotion and hard work on her part before he became reasonably civilised. The trouble with Roger was, he spent five years living in a flat with three other medical students before marriage. They did not have a washing machine so they took their laundry home twice a term to their mothers.

Roger smiles in a fond fashion at the happy memory.

'Yes!' he reminiscences, 'Dot doesn't understand this. In those days I was poor. I only had three pairs of underpants. I used to wear them for two weeks on one side, then turn them over and get another week out of them, then take them home for Mum to wash. She never complained. And it had the advantage of being practical and economical. Take what happens nowadays. Dot keeps losing socks in the wash. It doesn't matter how many pairs I have, once they've gone through her mincing process I end up with odd socks. You can have too much washing, too much cleanliness, too much tidiness you know.

'In the old days I could always find a pair of socks. It was on the floor with the rest of the clothes I took off last night. And I must say, that simple lifestyle gave a new meaning to the old saying "Roger, over and out."'

Why is it that the majority of men bring so many bad habits to marriage? They drift along in a daze, leaving unmade beds, dishes in the sink, dirty and clean washing in heaps on the floor, the place covered with filth and gunge, then if a woman makes a reasonable request like, 'Please do not use all the towels in the bathroom at once and leave them in a sodden heap on the floor so that there is nothing clean and dry left for me to use', she will be ignored.

Daph and I firmly believe that men begin life by ignoring their mothers. We feel that it gives a man a sense of being loved if he hears a female voice continually chittering away in the background. This appears to make him feel secure so he does not listen. He becomes expert at 'switching off' and has a useful weapon at hand. If needled and made to feel guilty he can always accuse his wife of nagging. By definition a wife who makes a reasonable request twice is a nag.

One day Kay and I were sitting drinking coffee by the fire when I moaned, 'I simply can't keep up with the rate himself uses towels. Whenever I go into the bathroom there is a sodden heap in the middle of the floor. The other day I ended up attempting to dry myself on a face cloth!'

Kay smiled, 'Perhaps he likes damp towels? Why don't you give him what he wants?'

'What do you mean?' I asked. 'How could he like damp towels?'

'He must love them because he gets them all wet and makes no attempt to dry them. Now, be reasonable, Doreen. He loves you. He would not set out deliberately to annoy you. He's not stupid, so he must realise that he's leaving wet towels for you. In the deep inner recesses of his mind he must believe you are similar to him and like wet towels. If I were you I'd give him what he wants, wet towels. What does he do if he takes a bath and finds all the towels sitting soaking on the floor?'

'He shouts and asks if I'd get him a clean one.' I replied.

'So he can make it wet for you! Isn't that good of him?'

'What?! I don't see it that way! I'm at my wit's end. He won't confine himself to two towels at once, then hang them up and I'm becoming demented. I can't keep up with the washing and I don't know what to do!'

'Easy!' replied Kay. ' The next time himself takes a bath make sure the towels are in their usual place, soaking on the bathroom floor. If necessary cheat a bit. Use all the towels yourself before he has a chance to get near them. Don't hang them up, just bung them on the floor and sprinkle water on them. Make sure they're the wettest, most uncomfortable towels in creation. Hide any clean towels and put the rest in the washing machine. When he asks for a towel just go into the bathroom and ask him what he means, asking for a towel when there are plenty on the floor.'

'He'll hit the roof!'

'Sure he'll hit the roof. Just smile at him sweetly and say, "I thought you liked towels like that. You always leave the towels there, like that, for me. I know you love me and wouldn't try to annoy me, so that must be the way you like towels. I'm a good wife. I want you to be happy so I'm helping you have things the way you like them. The rest of the towels are in the wash. I'll not bother drying them. That's a waste of time as you don't like dry towels. I'll just bring them in here and throw them on the floor when they're clean.'

To do him justice, he laughed and he has been more careful with towels since that day.

He has learnt to be tidy since I 'helped' him get the house in a real mess!

God love him, he was very busy working full time and doing a part-time degree. He buried the house in books, papers, notes, coffee spoons, mugs, crumbs and finally clothes. He was so busy he just rushed from one thing to another, dropping his possessions wherever he had finished with them. I ran around like the proverbial blue arsed fly trying to keep the place organised.

I like things to be tidy because they are easy to find, so I nearly went crazy, then I remembered Kay's wise advice. If that's the way he makes it, that's the way he wants it. Sock it to him, his way!

A golden opportunity arose one fine Saturday morning when himself went on a course and small daughter and I were left alone in the house. She was at that stage where she wanted to play with all her toys at once and she liked them all over the floor. I decided to help her make a real mess. I began to sew, dropping pieces of material, threads, spools and so on over the floor. The weather became warm and sunny so I decided to sunbathe while finishing my sewing outside. I went and changed into my bathing costume leaving my clothes strewn where they fell as I cast them off in abandoned fashion. Small daughter followed suite. Dishes were left on the table, the sink became cluttered with pots, the bathroom floor was littered. The place looked as if it had been hit by a bomb. I felt really proud of my efforts. Then the minister called!

I find the unerring instincts of members of the cloth amazing. You can have loads of suitable things to eat, the house organised, spotless, full of flowers, the smell of percolating coffee around for weeks and not one will come near you, but have a bad hair day, get into a mess, have only one soggy biscuit in the biscuit tin and there he will be, smiling on the door step! It does not matter what their religious persuasion is, they all have the same instincts. My minister was a Protestant, but, Sean and Ann have the most awful recollection of the parish priest's first visit shortly after their marriage.

Ann lived at home until the day she got married. Her parents were straight-laced and she was repressed. She did not appear to smoke, drink or go to discos and she went to bed early so her mind would be fresh for work next day. Suddenly, when she came home from her honeymoon it struck her, 'I'm free! Free! FREE! I can do what I want! I'm free! I wonder what it feels like to be drunk? I'm going to get plastered.'

Sean, who had had a more liberal upbringing tried to dissuade her.

'I've been drunk,' he explained, 'It's nothing to write home about. You risk being sick and having one hell of a headache next day.'

Ann said she would try to drink enough to make her feel good and not enough to make her sick, but she wanted the experience, so the next Friday night they got a take-a-way, a video and a carryout. They sat in their cosy living room watching the video and getting sozzled. After a while Ann began to giggle.

'What are you laughing at?' asked Sean.

'I was just thinking,' replied Ann, 'Now that we're married I have endowed you with all my worldly goods and you have done the same to me.'

'That's right,' replied Sean, puzzled, 'So?'

'So my knickers are your knickers!' giggled Ann, 'And I own your pants! Get them off! I want to wear them. I'll let you wear my knickers.'

'I don't want to wear your knickers,' replied Sean, who was staying reasonably sober to keep an eye on her. 'I would rather wear my own pants.'

'They aren't your pants, they're my pants. We're married so I own all the pants in the house and you own all the knickers.'

She took all her clothes off and climbed on top of the piano with her drink in one hand and her underwear in the other. She sat on the piano waving her drink and her underwear chanting 'Sean's knickers! Sean's knickers!' when the door bell rang. The parish priest had come round to congratulate the young couple.

Ann never got drunk again so perhaps the motto, 'Sock it to him, his way' also applies to women.

We're married, so my knickers are your knickers!

PAYING THE GUESS BILL
by
Billy Simpson

The fear of woman is the basis of good health
— Spanish Proverb

Women are roundabout creatures. They can't tell you anything directly. It's always "Guess who called today?" Or "Guess how much the fridge repair cost?" etc.

And a man stands there like a contestant in some fool quiz show making mad guesses. The worst of these guessing games they throw at you is the dreaded "Do you notice anything different?"

Why do they do that? Why can't they just tell you straight out that they've dyed their hair green? Why does everything have to be a test? They already know that men are not the most observant species.

And these games aren't even spontaneous. They do it deliberately just to keep you off-balance. Enjoying our dismay and the sight of our heads swivelling around like a car doll as we frantically search for the elusive difference before the penalty clause is invoked.

It has to be admitted, however, that a husband will never fall into the doomed category of the "info-underclass" (to coin the latest techno-ailment.)

Apparently the info-underclass are folk excluded from the information highway on the computer net.

A woman comes into marriage already chock-full of information and advice. And she will let you have all of it. Some free - but some you'll have to pay the "Guess Bill" to get.

CAN'T YOU SEE MY HAIR IS GREEN?!!!!
by
Doreen McBride

A husband is what's left of a lover after the nerve has been extracted
– Helen Rowland

Billy asks, 'Why can't a woman just say she has dyed her hair green and not go in for guessing games, such as "Guess what's different about me? Why can't she realise that men aren't the most observant of creatures?"'

I think the answer is to do with the fact that women tend to overestimate men. It is all to do with lust and the wooing process. When the average man first sets eyes on a woman he fancies his eyes light up. He sees a large green sign for GO within the deep recesses of what passes as his mind. This does something magical to his make-up. Within seconds he has learnt to have an intelligent conversation, to be loving and attentive, he becomes genuinely interested in what the object of his desires thinks, he finds her hobbies fascinating. If she buys a new handkerchief he will notice and new clothes, shoes and hair styles send him into raptures of praise. In other words he acts like a normal woman. He is a good companion. He displays many talents and himself was no exception (neither, according to Daph, was Billy). During our courting days himself wrote poetry for me and sang softly, with a sexy French accent, in my ear as we danced. Now-a-days, for goodness sake, he cannot even dance!

Having wooed and won his love, men then go back to normal - inarticulate, unobservant and lacking in intelligence. This is a terrible shock to the average woman's system. She cannot believe that her romantic Latin lover has turned into Fred Bloggs, who snores, breaks wind and grunts. She cannot believe that those smelly socks and stained underwear were wrested from the body of her one-time Romeo. It is a truly traumatic experience. She is traumatised by the thought that her lover was bluffing and keeps hoping that the essential 'him' still exists under that thick hide. So what does she do?

All human beings, men and children included, will attention seek if the object of their affection ignores them. A man, once he has gratified his desires, ignores his woman, so she, in these circumstances and in common with the rest of humanity, will attention seek. She will, for instance, dye her hair green. She will not want to appear condescending by saying, 'Look! I have dyed my hair green!' That inevitably leads to the object of her affection being placed in the position where he can wrong foot her because her one time lover will undoubtedly reply, 'Do you think I'm stupid? Of course I see you have dyed your hair green. It's obvious isn't it?' On the other hand, if she does not mention the obvious change that will probably lead to trouble. It is a catch twenty-two situation.

Himself lived in a flat in a large Victorian house when we first got married. We had a large bedroom, with high ceilings, drafty windows and doors and no central heating. It was a cold comfortless place altogether and our few sticks of furniture got lost in the wide open spaces. I was never satisfied with the way it looked so I kept hauling the furniture around in an attempt to disguise the fact that the carpet only covered a fraction of the floor, leaving a large expanse of drafty painted floorboards around it. One day I worked really hard, pushing and shoving, hauling and heaving, cleaning and polishing until I was satisfied that the grim place looked as good as possible. That evening himself and I went to visit friends, then I went to bed while he finished reading the paper.

I was half-asleep when himself came rushing up the stairs in

a great state of excitement. Teachers had been awarded a pay
rise. It was for some exotic amount, like £30 pounds a year, which
in those far off days actually made a difference. I too became
excited and sat up in bed while we discussed what we would do
with the comparative riches. Life was going to be wonderful!
Himself undressed as we talked and went to where the bed had
been the previous night. I had time for the thought to flash through
my mind, 'Surely he can't be going to attempt to get into bed in
its old place?' He did! He sat down heavily on the floor and yelled,
'Where the hell's the bed? And where the hell are you?' He looked
up, saw me and asked, 'Why didn't you tell me you'd shifted the
bed?'

'I thought you'd notice,' I replied, 'its so obvious. Why didn't
you see the bed was in a different place? I'm in it and you were
talking to me.'

'Humph!' himself grumped, rubbing his sore bottom, 'I don't
think to ask you if the floor is under my feet when I get up in the
morning, so why should I have to ask you about the position of
the bed when I get into it at night?

Now, like all other woman, I play games. 'Guess what I've
done?' It is safer. There is only one occasion when I absolutely
REFUSE to play this type of game and that is when we are staying
in our weekend cottage.

The cottage has single beds. Sometimes I feel cold, or lonely,
in the middle of the night so I sneak in beside himself, for a
warm up, or a cuddle. If he realises that I am invading his bed he
screams, beats his arms about and shouts, 'Get out! Go away!
Clear off!'

The first time this happened I felt very hurt. 'Why?' I asked,
'Why did you shout at me when I sneaked into bed beside you?'

The answer was quite simple. 'I thought you were the dog.'

Our latest dog, Sunny, is a white toy poodle. Never in my wildest dreams would I have thought that himself could mix me up with the dog.

Sunny was born in Rasharkin. He is a dog of character with a wild dash of Irish blood coursing his veins. Like all creatures endowed with a touch of the Irish he has a very good understanding of the law, which, if he considers it stupid, he disobeys. Sunny knows he is not allowed into bed, a law which he considers silly, unreasonable and worth ignoring, so he, like me, has a tendency to sneak in beside himself in the wee small hours of the morning. Himself objects to sleeping with the dog, so yells discouragement at him. I have suggested that it is unreasonable to mix up your wife with a toy poodle. Himself thinks differently. He says he cannot tell the difference between us because we both have cold noses and white hair. Faced with this great lack of powers of observation I REFUSE to ask, 'Guess who's getting into bed beside you? Me or the dog?'

I refuse to ask, 'Guess who's getting into bed beside you?'

THE ULTIMATE IN STYLE AND DISCOMFORT
by
Billy Simpson

*A woman who takes her husband about with her everywhere is like a
cat that goes on playing with a mouse long after she has killed it*
– Saki

Imelda Marcos and every woman who ever lived are sisters under
the skin when it comes to shoes. They may lament that they
haven't a shoe to their foot but if a husband opens any bedroom
cupboard door he will be buried in an avalanche of ladies
footwear.

In terms of walking distance covered by any pair of ladies'
shoes during their lifetime, the mileage-per-sole is not high. Some
make only one or two trips before being consigned to that great
graveyard in the wardrobe. Manufacturers get rich, not from
wearing shoes but from women burying them.

It's the Coleman's mustard syndrome. More is washed off
plates than ever gets spread on food.

And with women, comfort is not a plus point in footwear.
Any day you will see women limping along in shoes designed to
direct the entire body weight onto the big toe. Impractical
contraptions that may be high style but appear to have been
designed by someone who had never actually seen a woman's
foot close to.

They are a bit like a man's foot, only smaller and have five
toes each. Not just one big pointed one.

Most of the cheap flat sandals bought on any one day probably
sell to women who can't walk another step on the beautiful

instruments of torture they'd put on in the morning to go shopping.

If any husband inflicted as much pain on his wife as she does on herself with impractical footwear, he'd be locked away.

The difference between a man and a woman buying shoes is not just in the contrasting time-scales of the transactions. It has also to do with basic motivation.

As a bachelor I was only moved to buy new shoes if the old ones started taking on water. Or the sole got so thin I could step on a coin and know if it was heads or tails.

I think it was just after we got engaged that Daph first happened to be with me when I was buying shoes. I went in, asked for a pair of brown shoes, size eight, broad fitting. The salesman brought a pair. I tried them on. They were reasonably comfortable. I bought them, kept them on and dumped the old ones in a bin.

It was one of the few times I'd ever seen the woman speechless. She kept opening and closing her mouth like she had something to say but was too shocked to say it. Eventually she gasped something like "Is that all you are going to try on?" Like I'd just broken some kind of holy retail taboo and was risking the wrath of the great shoe god Kantmakup Memindus.

However, men of my generation were a bit like that. As long as shoes were comfortable and kept your feet dry, why waste your time hanging round shoe stores. We had this theory that nobody was going to be looking at our feet, since we never looked at anybody else's.

Of course this is a state of innocence that marriage rudely shatters.

I confess to experiencing my own sense of shock the first time I accompanied Daph on a shoe-buying mission and lost a whole day of my life. Not that she has ever found exactly what she wants in a shoe, but buys some anyway rather than go home without a parcel.

Over the last 30 years I have had many lost days being dragged along on her shoe quests. It occurred to me that those men you read about who are obsessed with female footwear to the point of therapy or police custody will never come close to the intensity of how women feel about shoes. Footwear is their narcotic. If some Evangelist came along promising a Heaven shaped like a big shoe with tall heels many would convert tomorrow.

What women have succeeded in doing is changing man's own motivation for buying shoes. I suspect that, like many husbands, any personal shoe purchases made latterly have had little to do with necessity. More likely a vain attempt to alleviate the boredom of waiting around while your wife continues her life-long mission to seek out new shoes and boldly go where no toe has gone before.

I suspect science fiction writers got the idea for the time-space continuum from their wives and the mysterious elastic five minutes.

That five minutes that expands to accommodate the mood of a woman caught somewhere between shopping frenzy and chronic indecision.

There will be a lot of it about over the coming weeks as women all over the country are telling husbands and boyfriends "You wait here, I'm just popping into this shop for five minutes."

Given the choice between waiting in a mall or going back to the car, a man should always choose the car. Hanging around a mall looking at other weary men caught in the same elastic five minute trap is depressing.

Especially the really sad ones who have gone catatonic from tannoys chirping "For the convenience of shoppers, Smoking is not permitted in this mall," before suffering serious brain damage.

I have often thought the Department of Statistics should issue men with the mean averages of how long it will take a woman to buy certain items. A pair of shoes, a dress, a gift or a card. And make them available on Ceefax. This would give us an approximate idea of just how long five minutes is in woman-speak.

Just give us a hint. Don't leave us in limbo, afraid to go for a dander round the bookshops in case she suddenly pops out of the shop and assumes you've been run over.

Why do women always assume that a man who is a little late has been run over? I can't remember the number of times a woman has snapped at me "Where were you? I thought you'd been run over."

Why do they say things like that? Especially in a mall where the worst that could happen is getting dented by a wayward shopping trolley. Painful, perhaps, but hardly as dramatic as getting melled by a bus.

Women often get impatient with men who stand around looking at their watches and exhaling sighs that have a lot of martyr in them.

"Why don't you go and wait in the car," they snap, "and I'll see you there in five minutes."

So you go to the car and sit there with a lot of other sad souls, steaming up their windscreens with their martyr sighs.

You fiddle with the radio, searching for a station that isn't playing Rap or diddle-dee-dee music. Usually it is a toss up between the afternoon play on Radio 4, or muttering the answers to questions on some DJ's general knowledge quiz that could have won you a T-Shirt if you could be bothered to phone.

So you resort to people watching. I remember one Christmas, sitting in the car waiting for Daph to return from one of her panic buying expeditions, when a car pulled in beside me, screeched to a halt and a flustered woman stepped out.

"Now," she said to someone in the car, "just you wait there quietly Timmy and mummy will be back in five minutes."

I assumed it was a small child she was talking to because I couldn't see anyone in the passenger seat. But as she hurried away, the head of a worried looking King Charles Spaniel appeared at the window.

We exchanged sympathetic looks. Neither of us bought that "five minutes" story.

There is also something spooky about a woman's ability to disappear when it suits her. I expect every husband has had the experience of walking along the street talking to his wife, when people start looking at him oddly.

He turns around and realises he is alone and giving the appearance of one talking to himself.

In my own case I just retrace my steps back along the street until I come to a shoe shop where Daph is usually found hopping around on one foot trying on some footwear from the rack.

They never tell you they are leaving. They simply disappear. Like Harrison Ford's wife in that film where she got kidnapped in Paris. When Harrison was going demented trying to find her, I was tempted to shout at the screen "Try the shoes shops!."

ONLY GOOD FOR SHOPPING AND YAPPING?

by

Doreen McBride

The great, and almost only comfort about being a woman is that one can always pretend to be more stupid than one is and no-one is surprised.

−Freya Stark

It has often been said that behind every successful man there is a good woman. This is just as true today as it was in the past, although life has become more difficult for married women as they have to work and carry the main responsibility for home-making. So why does the typical man speak of women in such derogatory terms? It is not logical. I used to find the sort of thing men say annoying, now, like Daph, I just shrug my shoulders and think to myself, men must feel inferior or they would not have to spout rubbish, such as 'Women are only good for shopping and yapping.'

Daph says men make up lies about women to hide their own inadequacies and I agree with her. She thinks the list of lies perpetuated by men about women is endless and very deep-rooted in our society. I have discovered it also applies to female dogs, although it took my daughter, who was then four years of age, to point that out.

One day we were walking in the park. We had our much loved, petted poodle pooch, Mitzi ,on a lead. As we walked along the tree-lined path admiring the golden daffodils an elderly lady approached. She, like us, was obviously enjoying the fresh spring air. She stopped, smiled and began to chat. Mitzi went over and began sniffing around her flat sturdy leather shoes. The old lady bent down and began to pet my poodle.

'Is that a bitch?' she asked.

'Yes.' I replied.

My daughter stood there, every inch of her stature shaking with indignation. 'Mummy,' she complained as we moved away, 'You said Mitzi's a bitch.'

'Yes dear,' I replied, 'so I did.'

'That's a terrible thing to say! Mitzi's a nice dog.'

'Yes!' I explained. 'She IS a nice dog, but she's a lady dog and lady dogs are called bitches.'

'Why?' came the quick response.

'Because that's the proper name for a female dog.'

Four year olds are very probing in their questioning. I would rather face a judge and jury any day.

'Why are lady dogs called bitches?' she repeated.

'I don't really know.' I replied. 'I've never really thought about it. Why do you think they shouldn't be called bitches?'

'Because "bitch" isn't a nice name.'

'It's not nice if you call a lady a bitch, but it's different for dogs. Bitch is a perfectly respectable name for female dogs.'

'Do boy dogs have a nasty name?' she asked. 'What do you call a boy dog?'

'You just call it a dog.'

'That's awful?!' she insisted, looking close to tears at the imagined insult and injustice to her much loved pet.

I felt curious. 'Why do you think it's awful to call a lady dog a bitch?' I asked.

'It's not fair,' she explained, 'because poor Mitzi is a nice modest dog. When she wants to go potty she squats down quietly and doesn't show anything to anybody. You just think what boy dogs do! They stand on three legs and wave themselves about against lamp-posts and things. You can see everything they've got. They don't care. It's not a bit nice yet humans don't call them nasty names like bitches!'

Yes! Daph is right. The rot in our society which causes innocent females to be called names runs very deep. Men should attempt to understand the female psyche, to realise and feel flattered because of women's deep–seated desire to please them (by appearing as attractive as possible) which leads to angst over buying such things as shoes and visits to the hairdressers.

'It's not fair, lady dogs are called bitches'

DANGER - WRONGED WOMAN AHEAD
by
Billy Simpson

Many a man in love with a dimple makes the mistake
of marrying the whole girl
— Stephen Leacock

FIRST PRINCIPLE OF CLOSE ENCOUNTERS -"The probability of meeting someone you know increases when you're with someone you don't want to be seen with."

A husband with a roving eye is not unusual. The risky bit is where he lets other parts of his anatomy go roving as well. In these days of information highways and information in-laws, infidelity is rarely a secret for long and a wife's wrath is not something you ever want to see. It can range from "Bobbiting" - as in John Wayne Bobbit who lost more than his heart when his wife got at him with the kitchen knife - to the even more deadly "Bravely standing by."

A little while ago I was seriously thinking of writing to film actor Hugh Grant advising him to dump that girl-friend of his.

I know that Mr. Grant, personable though he may be, had been a bit foolish with his lust life but his career seems to be recovering nicely again. Even booming.

What he does not need is a woman "bravely standing by him."

"Bravely standing by you" women are an extremely dangerous species. Usually they are standing by with a club. Particularly those who put on their solemn "bravely standing by" faces for the press photographers. You can almost hear the martyr's sigh coming off Liz Hurley's photograph.

This is not the face of a forgiving woman. This is the face of a woman who is going to turn this sad little sin into a Wagner opera.

Women who are not the standing-by types - the ones who come at you with a knife or push you off a cliff are preferable. They get it over with quickly and clear off.

The "Standing by" woman hangs around, convinced that killing is too good for you. She plans an extended guilt trip that has the smack of eternal damnation about it.

In most civilised legal systems, after going straight for a certain number of years, an ex-criminal can have his earlier indiscretions, wiped off his record.

"Standing-by" women regard this attitude as wishy-washy liberalism gone mad. Faced with a good domestic argument she not only drag up all your previous convictions (proven and imaginary) but remind you how she nobly stood by you in your time of need/disgrace/mid-life crisis/hangover or whatever.

The courts may have let Mr. Grant off with a modest fine but you get a life sentence from a "standing-by" woman.

It is her big chance to play Joan of Arc, the martyred bride, the wronged woman, the lover betrayed and as many other notes in the torch song as the violin will take.

And Miss Hurley, being a professional actress, might be able to give a performance that could grab the title of the world's "Top Wronged Woman" from the late Princess Diana.

Ever notice that it is always women who are "wronged" and always men who do the "wronging". This is one of the great myths of our time. I know plenty of chaps who have been "wronged" by flighty women but they get precious little sympathy. The politically correct attitude of the times being that if they're men they probably had it coming to them.

An attitude reinforced by the crop of TV documentaries where bitter women are given fifty minutes to an hour to sit around bitching about what brutes men are.

It is well known that there are women who would knock down five good men to throw herself at the feet of a heartless smoothie with a bit of charisma. The world is full of lonely men who can't get a girl because so many women prefer brutes who will break their hearts, steal their money or leave them holding the baby.

Then they go on television to tell the world that all men are the devil's spawn.

I will stand by my man

I'M NOT A DIRTY BRUTE! I'M JUST INTERESTED!
by
Doreen McBride

She's the kind of girl who climbed the ladder
of success wrong by wrong
– Mae West

For once I agree with Billy! He says a husband with a roving eye is not unusual. Actually I would put it a bit more strongly - every man has a roving eye and as long as he has an attitude such as, 'I've had a feast, now I'm just looking at the menu.' and keeps his other bits at home that is excusable as far as I am concerned.

The first time I realised that all men are essentially dirty old men I was disconcerted and amazed.

It happened in London after himself and I had decided to spend a day apart following our individual interests. I returned, opened the bedroom door of our hotel and there he was, all alone, sitting on the bed, laughing his leg off.

He looked up. 'Had a good day?' he asked.

'Fine!' I replied, 'Interesting. Now you look as if you've either had a ball or gone stark, staring, raving mad. Why are you laughing?'

He looked a bit sheepish.

'Go on! Tell me. We're married after all. Did somebody tell you a dirty joke?'

'No! It's nothing.'

He started to shower and change his clothing, getting ready for a night on the town.. The big smoke of London can feel hot and sticky in July. He sat down heavily on the bed to don his socks and burst our spontaneously laughing. I started to laugh at him laughing and we rolled about, with the tears streaming down our cheeks.

'What are you laughing at?' he asked.

'I wish I knew!' I replied. 'I'm laughing at you laughing and I don't even know what you're laughing at.'

Eventually he told me the whole story, which caused me to become totally disillusioned and changed my basic beliefs in men. Daph says I should have known better, but in all honesty I was a complete innocent. This is the sorry tale he told me. He had been rushing back to the hotel to meet me when he saw a beautiful sight walking in front of him along the tunnel in the underground. She was young, shapely, smartly dressed in a black mini-skirt, high heeled shoes and black stockings. She had a wonderful shapely pair of legs that just went on and on. Marvellous they were, with a straight seam up the back. There were few people around so he loitered as she got on the escalator in front of him, because he **knew** when the moving stairway rose and reached his eye level he would be able to see up her skirt. He looked up in happy anticipation. Her legs were wonderful and as she went higher he saw further and had to contain himself. She had a big hole in her knickers!

I was horrified. To think that my beloved, who I had always considered reasonably pure, **knew** he could see up a woman's skirt on an escalator! I was shocked! Billy says I was behaving unreasonably by displaying symptoms of shock as that's just the kind of thing a man knows instinctively. Himself agrees while George says men are not 'dirty' as far as women are concerned, they are just 'interested' and John, who used to be a bus driver says every driver will automatically adjust his mirror to keep a fatherly eye on 'any hot piece of stuff' sitting at the back of the bus, particularly if she is wearing a short skirt and crosses her legs. He confesses to once being so interested in a girl that he travelled from Ballysillan to the City Hall in seven minutes flat and forgot to pick up any passengers!

Men really are funny creatures. Why are they so interested in women's anatomy? Women get by without hankering urges to look up men's trouser legs. What makes men different? I wish I knew.

The rot starts young as I remember seeing a group of small boys giggling at the bottom of Primary School stairs. They looked incredibly innocent as they turned their angelic eyes heavenwards. I wondered what was in their minds and looked around. At first I was puzzled, then light struck.

The school was being visited by a very attractive group of girls, Stranmillis education students about to embark on their first teaching practice. They were upstairs talking to the Vice-Principal and judging by their position they were about to walk down the stairs holding on to the bannister. The girls were wearing high heel shoes and full skirts so the boys at the lower level were in the ideal position to view their underwear as they descended!

Since realising that all men are 'interested' I have been very careful either to wear trousers or to walk on the stairway well away from open banisters, and mini skirts are definitely out. Men are not going to get gratuitous pleasure out of me! It is not good for them, indeed it can be positively dangerous as 38 year old Paul Shimkonis found when he held his stag night at the Diamond Dolls Club in Clearwater, Florida. An exotic dancer, called Tawny Peaks, with a spectacular bust, size 69HH, hit him on the head with her boobs so hard that he suffered a whip lash injury. Paul is suing Tawny Peaks for £10,000 as he says it was like being hit with two cement blocks and he has been in agony ever since.

THE DRAMA QUEEN SYNDROME
by
Billy Simpson

Next to the wound, what women make best is the bandage
– Jules Barabey d'Aurevilly

One of the first things a man discovers about women is that there is nothing so mundane, so trivial or so pathetically unimportant that a woman can't make an epic drama out of it.

This is the dangerous Drama Queen syndrome that afflicts women everywhere.

For such women there are no minor works - everything is "Macbeth" with the Complete Works thrown in.

You only have to listen to one woman talking to another on the telephone to realise they are incapable of understatement.

I remember trying to concentrate on a book once and hearing Daph exclaiming down the phone:

"OH MY GOODNESS!! I don't BELIEVE it! But that is OUTRAGEOUS! OH MY GOD!!!!!! That is FANTASTIC!!"

Now it is very hard to concentrate when someone is reacting like this to a piece of news you can't hear. You start wondering if the woman at the other end of the line is trapped in a phonebox by a mad rapist. Or her house is on fire. Or there is a thug at the door with a baseball bat.

Meanwhile Daph was continuing with her horror and astonishment, "That is INCREDIBLE!! . . . Well HONESTLY that is hard to credit! Isn't that just the DEAD END?" and "Wouldn't you just DIE???"

When she finally put down the phone my curiosity got the better of me and I said "What was all that about?"

"Ach nothing" she said, "just a bit of chat."

This strange ability to treat the trivial and the important to the same adjectives is one of the things that confuses men trying to communicate with the opposite sex. And makes you wonder why there aren't more female sports writers.

When a woman is in the mood to panic she demands a reciprocal amount of panic in a husband. Whether he feels like it or not. If you keep calm she is convinced you are doing it deliberately just to annoy her.

Now and then she'll awaken you in the middle of the night and ask you to perform some miracle that could get you canonised if you could do it.

Like the night of the great storm.

"Do you hear that gale?" she whispers.

My left eye fluttered half open.

I listened.

"Yes", I said and went back to sleep.

The next time the elbow struck rib it had all the subtlety of Bruce Lee's fist of fury.

"What.. What?" I spluttered, struggling to get conscious before I was attacked again.

"LISTEN" she commanded. "I've never heard anything like it."

I gave a few quick glap...glap...glaps... with my mouth to waken up my tongue and listened again. The wind was screaming like a banshee with its matrimonial prospects caught in a revolving door..

"Oh Aye, " I said.

Very bloody interesting. I settled back down .

"Did you not hear that terrible clatter on the roof ? "

"No. " I lied.

"Well, I thought the roof had come off . " she gasped dramatically, sitting up clutching the bedclothes to her neck .

"Did it?"

"No" she said, "but I think you should get up and do something. "

Do something? DO SOMETHING! ! ?

" Do WHAT ? "

"Something, " she insisted.

I explained, as patiently as I could, that I was not all that good at stopping storms and that she had obviously confused me with the Almighty.

"You could get up and see if we've any tiles off. " she huffed.

Great. Three in the morning. Pitch black. Rain battering the windows like Lambeg drumsticks. A hundred mile-an-hour gale sweeping all before it - and I'm supposed to run outside and try and catch flying tiles .

If a tile came off in that gale it could have been in Donaghadee before I knew about it. And if I got in its way I could have been in Donaghadee with it.

I turned over, thumped the pillow to make a head groove and settled down determined not to budge unless the roof took off and the house with it .

Daph threw back the bedclothes and clambered out.

Clump. Clump. Clump. Creak. Creak. Slam. Clump.

That wasn't the storm. It was she clumping round the house opening doors and looking out windows.

"Woof . Woof woof . "

"Aaaaaaah. Did the big bad storm frighten the wee man", came her voice from the kitchen, where she was comforting the Pekinese.

I gave up. Got up and staggered out of bed.

"That's wild out there, " she said, "The trees across the road are all bent over. "

"Probably lack of sleep" I said.

Anyway there were no broken windows or obvious damage. In the morning we found we'd lost a couple of ridge tiles. One was lying half way down the roof. We never found the other one. Probably clobbered some poor bloke in Donaghadee whose wife sent him outside to see if their roof was still on.

However that night taught me a valuable lesson. I learned that the next time a big storm was forecast to get in some sleeping pills. And slip a couple into her tea at supper-time when she wasn't looking.

THE DRAMATIC MAN
by
Doreen McBride

If love is the answer, could you please rephrase the question?
– Lily Tomlin

It is sad, but true, a man's idea of what is dramatic is very different from that of a woman.

If the washing machine breaks down, decides to boil the wash causing all the clothes inside to either shrink or become creased out of existence, then spews several gallons of water all over the floor, that according to any woman is a dramatic tragedy. The average man is remarkably resistant to learning how to use a washing machine so malfunctions in this area will be outside his ken. As he has not had to cope he will be entirely unmoved by the tragedy, unless one of his favourite shirts has been ruined, when he will blame his wife, not the machine!

If a woman has a mishap, such as that described above, she will turn to a female companion for solace and will receive comfort from conversations in terms of 'That was INCREDIBLE...' 'Wasn't that the DEAD END...' and 'Couldn't you just DIE!!!' And if any eavesdropping man asks, 'What was that all about?' He is bound to get an answer such as 'Nothing.' As far as he is concerned it would be 'nothing' and the wise woman will realise that it is a waste of time attempting to explain.

On the other hand, men become overexcited over trifles that would not cause a woman to turn a hair. Himself becomes very dramatic if he ever has to collect our poodle from the canine beauty parlour, an event any woman, including me, can take in her stride. He moans, to everyone who will listen, for weeks afterwards that it costs more to have the dog's hair cut than his! In vain I have pointed out that the dog's body is larger than his head and that Lisa should be paid extra for dealing with a greater, more time consuming area. Himself cannot see the sense in that statement, although, in all honesty, I do feel there could be hope for future generations of men and hope for the future of male logic in general because Andy, a younger man, commented to himself, 'Look here. . . I have to agree with what Doreen is saying. You are not comparing like with like. That dog has hair all over its body, not just on its head so Lisa is cutting the hair off its most private parts. Personally I wouldn't take fifty pound to cut the hair around your backside.'

The term 'dramatic' is an understatement if the average man suffers from a minor ailment, such as the common cold. Will he take a couple of aspirin and give the world peace by going to bed with a hot water bottle? Perish the thought! He has to moan, protesting loudly, red nosed, attention seeking, handkerchief in fist, sneezing, casting off millions of germs, doing his best to infect the rest of humanity.

Suffering man is dramatic about taking simple remedies, such as aspirin. He moans about the dangers of pill popping, insists he does not believe in medicines and never takes them, then demands to be given some sort of magic cure to make him instantly better. His method of dealing with a pill is dramatic and interesting. He looks woebegone with eyes resembling those of a large spaniel, places it in his mouth, takes a gulp of water, then shakes his head, resembling a dog killing a rat, in an attempt to overcome his perceived difficulty in swallowing.

If a woman gets a cold, her husband will tell her to cheer up. After all, it is only a cold. It is not serious and she should be capable of carrying on as normal, feeding the family, working a normal day and looking after the children. Of course she does not need medication! Pills are an evil device with dangerous side effects and should be avoided at all costs. Frankly I think women are faced with the burden of childbirth because the good God realised that men are such bad patients He decided to give His Head peace and give women the major task in regeneration.

Thank goodness the procedure today regarding childbirth has improved enormously over that offered in the past. At last medical science appears to acknowledge men have something to do with reproduction so they feel guilty if they are not present at the birth, this means that men are inclined to be more tactful about the effort required to produce an heir. I remember Pat's fury when Ron described the birth of their twins 'as easy as falling off a log'! She says he should have been there to see what occurred and that if her more sensitive private parts had not been stitched and trussed like those belonging to an oven ready chicken, so that she could hardly move, she would have gone home to her mother. Today, over thirty years later, she still bristles with indignation at the memory.

There is nothing on this earth that arouses a man's finally developed sense of the dramatic as his favourite sport. Think of the dramatic frenzy of football hooligans!

The effect of sport can be traumatic even if it does not reach the heights attained by the hooligans. I remember being entranced as I eavesdropped on two elderly women having lunch in Greyabbey. One said to the other, 'Lizzie, I feel desperate! I just don't know what to about our Sam and thon big edjiot next door. Every Saturday they go off to a match all full of happy anticipation, like a pair of kids. Then if their team wins they sit and celebrate by drinking all night and they have hangovers next day and are fit to bust. If their team loses they sit, blank, with faces like Lurgan spades and there's no living with them.

'Last Saturday I poked my head around the door and there were the two edjiots sitting drinking. I thought they were celebrating and said, "So your team won!" But, begad, they were drowning their sorrows. Apparently their team had been knocked out of the cup! Our Sam was so upset he dashed up the stairs and started throwing up rings round him. Now, nearly a week later he still isn't feeling right, he's that depressed.'

Personally I cannot understand what is so exciting about a lot of sweaty men, dressed in ridiculous shorts and inelegant baggy shirts, covered in mud, chasing an innocent ball around. It takes a man to get dramatic about it!

My team lost

THE LAST WORD

Oh, what a dear ravishing thing is the beginning of an Amour!
– Aphra Behn

Tara was tall, blonde with beautiful blue eyes and a figure the angels could envy. She smiled dreamily at the large sparkling diamond on her engagement finger.

'It's all going to be lovely! It will be the last word.' she said, 'The church will be filled with flowers and they are going to bring out the red carpet. I have a dreamy designer wedding gown, four bridesmaids, two flower girls and my sister's son, Jamie, is going to be a page boy and wear a kilt. He's little more than a baby and he's so cute!

'We're going to have the reception at home, film star style. Daddy has hired a big marquee to put on the lawn. It will be lovely, all filled with flowers and music. We're bringing the caterers in. They did my cousin's wedding and it was wonderful.

'We're going to Turkey for our honeymoon. Blue seas, golden sand! It'll be so romantic!'

On the wedding day the rain came down in stair rods. Tara got soaked going into the church and arrived up the aisle looking like a drowned rat. Cute little baby Jamie attempted to murder the flower girls during the reception, the marquee developed leaks, causing water to cascade down on the unfortunate guests, several of whom suffered from salmonella poisoning.

Tara and her new husband were not amused. In Turkey they both had 'Turkey trots' and spent the entire honeymoon in the bathroom squabbling over whose turn it was to use the facilities. The marriage lasted six months and they are now divorced.

If you are contemplating tying the knot remember it is

impossible to feel romantic while doing unromantic things such as washing dirty underwear, dealing with stomach bugs and suffering sleepless nights when baby has colic. Life is not smooth so marriage is bound to have its ups and downs, so make sure you can survive the nightmare as well as the dream.

Doreen's mother was right when she said 'the essence of marriage is 'keeping your promises to each other, even if you don't feel like it.' Hang in there kid! It can only get worse!